PRINCEWILL LAGANG

From Me to We: A Guide to Marriage

First published by PRINCEWILL LAGANG 2023

Copyright © 2023 by Princewill Lagang

All rights reserved. No part of this publication may be reproduced, stored or transmitted in any form or by any means, electronic, mechanical, photocopying, recording, scanning, or otherwise without written permission from the publisher. It is illegal to copy this book, post it to a website, or distribute it by any other means without permission.

Princewill Lagang asserts the moral right to be identified as the author of this work.

First edition

This book was professionally typeset on Reedsy.
Find out more at reedsy.com

Contents

1	Introduction	1
2	Foundations of a Unified Partnership	3
3	The Art of Communication in Marriage	6
4	Navigating Conflict as a Team	9
5	Cultivating Intimacy and Emotional Connection	12
6	Balancing Individuality and Togetherness	15
7	Shared Responsibilities and Household Harmony	18
8	Nurturing Romance Throughout Marriage	21
9	Growing Together Through Life's Changes	24
10	Parenthood: A Joint Adventure	27
11	Weathering Challenges and Celebrating Triumphs	30
12	The Ongoing Journey of "We"	33

1

Introduction

In a world that often celebrates individualism and self-reliance, it's easy to overlook the transformative power of partnership and the journey from "Me" to "We." This book is an exploration of that journey—a journey that is both personal and universal, intimate and shared. It's an invitation to delve into the intricate process of building a strong marital bond, where two distinct individuals come together to form an unbreakable partnership.

The path from individuality to partnership is not just a change in relationship status; it's a profound evolution that requires patience, understanding, and a willingness to embrace vulnerability. Our society frequently emphasizes self-discovery and self-fulfillment, often unintentionally overshadowing the beauty of shared dreams, collective growth, and shared accomplishments.

As we embark on this journey, we'll navigate the intricate terrain of partnership—a landscape marked by communication challenges, compromise, and the delicate dance of merging two unique perspectives into a harmonious whole. This is not a journey without its obstacles; it's a pilgrimage that demands self-reflection, empathy, and the courage to let go of rigid notions of self in favor of the emergence of a united "We."

The pages ahead will weave together personal anecdotes, psychological insights, and practical advice, offering a roadmap for couples seeking to transcend the surface level of companionship and venture into the depths of profound togetherness. We'll uncover the dynamics that drive successful partnerships, delve into the art of active listening and effective communication, and explore the transformative potential of shared goals.

Ultimately, this book is an ode to love, resilience, and the strength that comes from merging two distinct narratives into one cohesive story. It's an exploration of the human capacity to evolve, adapt, and expand beyond the confines of the self. So, dear reader, as we begin this journey together, let's open our hearts to the possibility of transcending "Me" to become an unbreakable and harmonious "We."

Remember, every great partnership is a testament to the power of unity—a unity that propels us beyond our individual limitations and into a realm where "We" can achieve and conquer far more than "Me" ever could.

2

Foundations of a Unified Partnership

A strong and enduring marriage rests upon a foundation built with intention, care, and a shared vision. In this chapter, we delve into the essential elements that lay the groundwork for a unified partnership that can weather life's challenges and celebrate its joys.

Section 1: The Significance of Unity and Shared Goals

Subsection 1.1: The Power of Unity
The journey from "Me" to "We" begins with understanding the profound strength that comes from unity. Unity isn't about erasing individuality, but rather, it's a celebration of the unique qualities each partner brings to the table. We explore how unity fuels shared aspirations and amplifies personal growth.

Subsection 1.2: The Role of Shared Goals
Shared goals act as guiding stars for a partnership. They create a sense of purpose and direction, helping partners move forward together. We discuss the importance of setting both short-term and long-term goals, and how

aligning aspirations can foster deeper emotional connection.

Section 2: Building Blocks of a Strong Marriage

Subsection 2.1: Trust and Open Communication

Trust is the cornerstone of any relationship. We explore the necessity of open and honest communication as a means to build trust, resolve conflicts, and create an environment where vulnerability is welcomed.

Subsection 2.2: Mutual Respect and Empathy

Respect and empathy pave the way for understanding and harmony. We examine how acknowledging each other's feelings, thoughts, and perspectives strengthens the partnership's emotional fabric.

Subsection 2.3: Collaboration and Compromise

Partnerships thrive on collaboration and compromise. We discuss the art of finding middle ground, where both individuals contribute to decisions and solutions, reinforcing the notion that "We" are greater than the sum of "Me."

Subsection 2.4: Shared Values and Beliefs

Shared values provide a moral compass for the partnership. We delve into the significance of aligning fundamental beliefs, which can offer stability in times of uncertainty and guide choices that reflect the shared essence of the relationship.

Section 3: The Dynamics of Emotional Intimacy

Subsection 3.1: Emotional Vulnerability

True intimacy demands emotional vulnerability. We explore the courage it takes to share fears, dreams, and insecurities, fostering an environment where partners can support and uplift one another.

Subsection 3.2: Affection and Intimacy

Affection and physical intimacy deepen the emotional connection between partners. We discuss how nurturing both emotional and physical aspects of intimacy enhances the bond and maintains the spark over time.

In this chapter, we've laid the groundwork for understanding how unity, shared goals, and foundational elements contribute to a strong and unified partnership. As we proceed, we'll delve deeper into practical strategies and exercises that empower couples to strengthen these foundations, allowing their partnership to flourish into a fulfilling and lasting connection.

3

The Art of Communication in Marriage

Communication is the lifeblood of any successful marriage. In this chapter, we explore how effective communication forms the cornerstone of a thriving partnership, and we delve into techniques that promote open dialogue, empathy, and active listening.

Section 1: Understanding Communication's Vital Role

Subsection 1.1: Communication as the Key to Connection
Communication is more than just exchanging words—it's about fostering a deep connection. We discuss how the quality of communication directly impacts emotional intimacy and understanding between partners.

Subsection 1.2: Navigating Challenges Through Communication
Challenges are inevitable in any relationship. We examine how healthy communication can prevent conflicts from escalating and create a safe space for discussing sensitive topics.

Section 2: Techniques for Effective Communication

Subsection 2.1: Active Listening and Empathetic Responses

Active listening is the foundation of meaningful conversations. We explore techniques to truly hear and understand each other's perspectives, followed by empathetic responses that validate feelings and experiences.

Subsection 2.2: Nonviolent Communication

Nonviolent communication is a powerful tool for expressing emotions and needs without blame or criticism. We delve into the four-step process—observation, feeling, need, and request—and how it cultivates compassionate dialogue.

Subsection 2.3: Constructive Feedback and Critique

Constructive feedback helps partners grow together. We discuss the art of offering and receiving feedback in a way that promotes personal development and strengthens the bond.

Section 3: Nurturing Emotional Connection through Communication

Subsection 3.1: Sharing Dreams and Goals

Communication is the vehicle for sharing aspirations. We explore how discussing dreams and goals fosters unity by creating a shared vision for the future.

Subsection 3.2: Managing Conflict and Disagreements

Conflict resolution is a skill that can make or break a relationship. We offer strategies for approaching conflicts as opportunities for growth, rather than threats to the partnership.

Subsection 3.3: Celebrating Milestones and Gratitude

Communication isn't just for addressing challenges—it's also for celebrating achievements and expressing gratitude. We discuss the significance of acknowledging each other's successes and showing appreciation.

In this chapter, we've unveiled the essential role that effective communication plays in nurturing a strong marital bond. By understanding the art of active listening, empathetic responses, and constructive dialogue, couples can lay the groundwork for a partnership built on trust, understanding, and shared emotional connection. As we move forward, we'll continue to explore practical exercises and strategies that empower couples to become skilled communicators, enriching their relationship in the process.

4

Navigating Conflict as a Team

Conflict is an inevitable part of any relationship, but how we navigate it can either fracture or fortify our partnership. In this chapter, we delve into approaches for addressing conflicts constructively, using them as opportunities to deepen understanding and strengthen the marital bond.

Section 1: Recognizing Conflict as Growth

Subsection 1.1: Embracing Conflict as a Normal Aspect of Relationships

Conflict is a natural consequence of two unique individuals coming together. We explore how viewing conflict as a catalyst for growth can shift the perspective from fear to opportunity.

Subsection 1.2: The Dual Nature of Conflict

Conflict holds both challenges and potential. We discuss how navigating disagreements together can lead to increased intimacy and mutual understanding.

Section 2: Approaches to Constructive Conflict Resolution

Subsection 2.1: The Importance of Calm Communication

Effective conflict resolution starts with communication. We explore techniques for maintaining a calm demeanor, even in the heat of the moment, to facilitate productive conversations.

Subsection 2.2: Active Listening and Validation

Active listening continues to play a crucial role in conflict resolution. We delve into how validating each other's feelings and perspectives can create a foundation for finding common ground.

Subsection 2.3: Time-Outs and Space for Reflection

Sometimes, stepping back is the best way to move forward. We discuss the value of taking time-outs to cool down and reflect before engaging in conflict resolution.

Section 3: Strategies for Strengthening Bonds Through Conflict

Subsection 3.1: Compromise and Collaboration

Conflict resolution often requires finding middle ground. We explore how compromise and collaboration can lead to creative solutions that satisfy both partners' needs.

Subsection 3.2: Vulnerability and Transparency

Sharing our vulnerabilities fosters empathy and connection. We discuss how opening up about fears and insecurities can humanize the conflict and create space for understanding.

Subsection 3.3: Learning from Conflict and Moving Forward

Every conflict holds lessons. We explore how reviewing and learning from disagreements can enhance communication skills and lead to more effective conflict resolution in the future.

In this chapter, we've unraveled the complexities of conflict within a marriage. By recognizing conflict as a natural part of growth and applying constructive approaches to resolution, couples can transform conflicts into opportunities to deepen their connection. As we move forward, we'll continue to explore strategies and exercises that empower couples to approach conflicts as a team, united by a shared commitment to understanding and growth.

5

Cultivating Intimacy and Emotional Connection

Intimacy goes beyond physical closeness; it's the emotional tapestry that binds partners in a profound and enduring bond. In this chapter, we explore the various dimensions of intimacy within a marital relationship and offer techniques for nurturing emotional closeness and vulnerability.

Section 1: The Multifaceted Nature of Intimacy

Subsection 1.1: Emotional Intimacy
  Emotional intimacy is the foundation of a deep connection. We delve into how sharing feelings, thoughts, and dreams fosters an environment of trust and understanding.

Subsection 1.2: Physical Intimacy
  Physical closeness is an essential aspect of intimacy. We discuss how maintaining affection, romance, and sexual connection contributes to the emotional fabric of the partnership.

Subsection 1.3: Intellectual and Spiritual Intimacy

Shared interests and values create intellectual and spiritual connections. We explore how engaging in meaningful conversations and shared activities enriches the partnership.

Section 2: Techniques for Nurturing Emotional Closeness

Subsection 2.1: Quality Time and Presence

Creating space for undivided attention nurtures emotional closeness. We discuss the importance of quality time together and techniques for being fully present in each other's company.

Subsection 2.2: Practicing Vulnerability and Trust

Vulnerability is the gateway to deeper connection. We explore strategies for opening up about fears, insecurities, and past experiences, fostering a sense of safety and trust.

Subsection 2.3: Reflective Listening and Empathetic Responses

Intimacy thrives on understanding. We delve into how reflective listening and empathetic responses create a nurturing environment for partners to share their innermost thoughts.

Section 3: Strengthening the Marital Bond through Intimacy

Subsection 3.1: Shared Rituals and Traditions

Creating shared rituals and traditions strengthens the emotional connection. We discuss how cultivating meaningful rituals—whether daily, weekly, or annual—creates a sense of continuity and unity.

Subsection 3.2: Exploration and Adventure Together

Novel experiences spark excitement and growth. We explore how embarking on adventures, whether big or small, contributes to the sense of exploration within the partnership.

Subsection 3.3: Affection and Nonverbal Communication

Affectionate gestures convey love and care without words. We discuss the significance of nonverbal communication and ways to express affection through touch, eye contact, and gestures.

In this chapter, we've illuminated the diverse dimensions of intimacy and how they contribute to a strong marital connection. By embracing emotional intimacy, practicing vulnerability, and nurturing various facets of connection, couples can cultivate a deep and lasting bond that transcends the surface level of companionship. As we continue our journey, we'll uncover practical exercises and strategies that empower couples to enrich their emotional connection and embark on a path of profound togetherness.

6

Balancing Individuality and Togetherness

Finding the equilibrium between personal growth and shared experiences is a delicate art within a marriage. In this chapter, we explore the intricate dance of maintaining individuality while nurturing the bonds of togetherness, and offer strategies for harmonizing these aspects.

Section 1: Embracing Personal Growth Within the Partnership

Subsection 1.1: The Essence of Individuality
Individuality is the cornerstone of a strong partnership. We discuss how honoring each partner's unique aspirations and passions contributes to personal growth and a rich relationship.

Subsection 1.2: Fostering Supportive Autonomy
Balancing independence and unity requires supportive autonomy. We delve into how allowing each other space for personal pursuits fosters mutual encouragement and respect.

Section 2: Strategies for Nurturing Shared Experiences

Subsection 2.1: Creating a Shared Vision

A shared vision unites partners. We explore how collaboratively setting goals and dreams fosters a sense of purpose and direction for the relationship.

Subsection 2.2: Carving Out Quality Time Together

Amid busy lives, quality time is precious. We discuss techniques for prioritizing shared moments, ensuring that togetherness remains an integral part of the partnership.

Subsection 2.3: Exploring New Horizons as a Duo

Exploration enriches the bond. We delve into the benefits of embarking on new experiences together, which not only create lasting memories but also deepen connection.

Section 3: Strategies for Maintaining Individual Identity

Subsection 3.1: Personal Time and Hobbies

Maintaining personal time and hobbies nourishes individuality. We explore how having dedicated moments for oneself contributes to a sense of self within the partnership.

Subsection 3.2: Open Communication about Needs and Desires

Communication is the bridge between individuality and togetherness. We discuss the importance of openly discussing each partner's needs, desires, and boundaries.

Subsection 3.3: Respecting Differences and Autonomy

Respecting differences is vital. We explore how recognizing and appreciating each other's unique qualities fosters an environment where individuality flourishes.

In this chapter, we've unraveled the intricacies of balancing personal growth and shared experiences within a marriage. By embracing individuality, nurturing shared visions, and maintaining open communication, couples can navigate the delicate balance between being "Me" and becoming a harmonious "We." As we continue our journey, we'll uncover practical exercises and strategies that empower couples to cultivate a partnership that thrives on both individuality and togetherness.

7

Shared Responsibilities and Household Harmony

A smoothly functioning household is the result of effective collaboration and shared responsibilities. In this chapter, we delve into the art of managing roles as a united team, fostering open communication, and creating an environment of household harmony.

Section 1: The Power of Collaboration in Household Management

Subsection 1.1: Approaching Household Responsibilities as a Team
Household responsibilities are a joint effort. We explore how treating tasks as shared responsibilities, rather than individual duties, promotes unity and balance.

Subsection 1.2: Redefining Traditional Gender Roles
Breaking free from traditional gender roles enriches the partnership. We discuss how embracing flexibility in roles and responsibilities supports a sense of equality and respect.

Section 2: Communication and Delegation in Household Management

Subsection 2.1: Open Communication about Needs and Preferences

Effective communication is vital. We delve into the importance of discussing individual needs, preferences, and expectations to avoid assumptions and misunderstandings.

Subsection 2.2: Delegating Tasks and Playing to Strengths

Delegation plays a key role in efficiency. We explore techniques for assigning tasks based on each partner's strengths and interests, fostering a sense of contribution.

Subsection 2.3: Regular Check-Ins and Adjustments

Flexibility is essential in household management. We discuss the significance of regular check-ins to assess the division of responsibilities and make adjustments as needed.

Section 3: Fostering Household Harmony Through Collaboration

Subsection 3.1: Setting Clear Expectations

Clarity prevents conflicts. We explore how setting clear expectations and discussing them openly ensures that both partners are on the same page.

Subsection 3.2: Appreciation and Acknowledgment

Acknowledging efforts enhances harmony. We discuss the value of showing gratitude for each other's contributions, creating an atmosphere of mutual appreciation.

Subsection 3.3: Problem-Solving as a Team

Challenges are opportunities for growth. We explore problem-solving strategies that involve both partners, reinforcing the idea that overcoming obstacles is a united effort.

In this chapter, we've uncovered the intricacies of managing shared responsibilities and fostering household harmony within a marriage. By approaching tasks as a team, maintaining open communication, and appreciating each other's efforts, couples can create an environment where household management becomes a collaborative and fulfilling endeavor. As we move forward, we'll continue to explore practical exercises and strategies that empower couples to harmonize their responsibilities and strengthen their partnership.

8

Nurturing Romance Throughout Marriage

Romance is the heartbeat of a marriage, infusing it with vitality and keeping the flame of passion burning bright. In this chapter, we explore the art of reigniting and sustaining romantic sparks over the course of a marriage, and offer creative ways to keep the flame of passion alive and well.

Section 1: The Essence of Romance in Marriage

Subsection 1.1: The Lifeline of Emotional Connection
Romance is the bridge to emotional intimacy. We discuss how nurturing romantic gestures fosters a sense of connection and deepens the bond between partners.

Subsection 1.2: The Evolution of Romance in Long-Term Relationships
Romance evolves over time. We explore how the expression of love transforms, and why consistent effort is key to maintaining the romantic

spark.

Section 2: Techniques for Reigniting Romance

Subsection 2.1: Prioritizing Quality Time Together
Quality time kindles romance. We discuss techniques for carving out moments of connection, whether through planned dates, spontaneous outings, or quiet evenings at home.

Subsection 2.2: Thoughtful Gestures and Surprises
Thoughtful gestures keep the excitement alive. We delve into the power of surprises—both big and small—and their ability to evoke feelings of appreciation and joy.

Subsection 2.3: Rediscovering Shared Interests
Shared interests rejuvenate the connection. We explore how revisiting hobbies and passions from early in the relationship can reignite shared excitement.

Section 3: Strategies for Sustaining Romance

Subsection 3.1: Open Communication about Desires
Communication is the heartbeat of romance. We discuss the importance of openly discussing desires, fantasies, and preferences to ensure that both partners feel valued.

Subsection 3.2: Intimacy and Physical Connection
Physical intimacy is a cornerstone of romance. We explore how maintaining physical closeness, affection, and sexual connection keeps the flame of passion alive.

Subsection 3.3: Regular Retreats and Getaways
Retreats breathe new life into romance. We discuss the benefits of periodic

getaways—whether a weekend escape or a longer vacation—to refresh the relationship.

In this chapter, we've illuminated the significance of nurturing romance throughout the course of a marriage. By prioritizing quality time, embracing thoughtful gestures, and sustaining open communication, couples can keep the flame of passion alive and thriving. As we continue our journey, we'll uncover practical exercises and strategies that empower couples to create an enduring atmosphere of romance, ensuring that the love between them remains vibrant and enduring.

9

Growing Together Through Life's Changes

Life is a journey of continuous change, and navigating these transitions as a united team is crucial to a strong marriage. In this chapter, we explore the impact of major life transitions on marital dynamics and offer strategies for adapting and growing as a couple through various life stages.

Section 1: Embracing Change as a Catalyst for Growth

Subsection 1.1: Recognizing the Inevitability of Change
Change is a constant in life. We discuss how acknowledging its inevitability creates a mindset of adaptability and helps partners approach transitions with a united front.

Subsection 1.2: The Role of Resilience in Facing Challenges
Resilience is vital in times of change. We delve into the power of resilience in maintaining emotional stability and supporting one another through life's

ups and downs.

Section 2: Navigating Major Life Transitions Together

Subsection 2.1: The Impact of Parenthood on Marriage
   Parenthood reshapes dynamics. We explore how becoming parents influences the partnership and discuss strategies for maintaining connection amid the demands of raising a family.

Subsection 2.2: Balancing Career Changes and Relationship Needs
   Career changes can affect relationships. We discuss how to balance pursuing individual career aspirations while also nurturing the relationship's needs and goals.

Subsection 2.3: Coping with Empty Nest Syndrome
   The empty nest phase brings its own challenges. We explore how couples can navigate the transition when children leave home and rekindle their connection in new ways.

Section 3: Strategies for Adapting and Growing as a Couple

Subsection 3.1: Regular Check-Ins and Reflections
   Check-ins foster connection. We discuss the value of periodic reflections and discussions to assess how each partner is coping with changes and to align future goals.

Subsection 3.2: Mutual Support and Encouragement
   Support is the foundation of growth. We explore how partners can provide emotional support and encouragement to each other, even when facing personal challenges.

Subsection 3.3: Embracing Shared Adaptation
   Adapting as a team strengthens unity. We discuss how shared adaptation

to life's changes—whether they are expected or unexpected—solidifies the partnership.

In this chapter, we've explored the transformative nature of major life transitions and how they impact marital dynamics. By embracing change as an opportunity for growth, maintaining open communication, and supporting one another through various life stages, couples can navigate challenges with resilience and come out stronger as a result. As we continue our journey, we'll uncover practical exercises and strategies that empower couples to evolve together, ensuring that their partnership remains strong and adaptable through life's ever-changing landscape.

10

Parenthood: A Joint Adventure

Parenthood is a transformative journey that requires unity, communication, and shared responsibilities. In this chapter, we delve into approaches for parenting as a united partnership, and strategies for balancing roles, communication, and the responsibilities that come with raising a family.

Section 1: Approaching Parenthood as a Unified Team

Subsection 1.1: Embracing Parenthood as a Joint Adventure
Parenting is a shared endeavor. We discuss the significance of approaching parenthood as a united front, fostering a sense of teamwork and cooperation.

Subsection 1.2: The Power of Co-Parenting
Co-parenting strengthens bonds. We explore how active participation and involvement from both partners contribute to a harmonious and balanced parenting dynamic.

Section 2: Balancing Roles and Responsibilities

Subsection 2.1: Defining Parenting Roles and Expectations

Clarity in roles prevents conflicts. We delve into the importance of openly discussing parenting roles and expectations, ensuring both partners are on the same page.

Subsection 2.2: Sharing Responsibilities Equitably

Equitable sharing promotes unity. We discuss strategies for dividing parenting responsibilities based on each partner's strengths, interests, and availability.

Subsection 2.3: Supporting Each Other's Parenting Styles

Parenting styles can differ. We explore how understanding and supporting each other's approaches to parenting enriches the partnership and benefits the children.

Section 3: Nurturing Communication and Connection

Subsection 3.1: Open Communication About Parenting Goals

Communication is key in parenting. We discuss the importance of discussing parenting goals, discipline methods, and long-term aspirations to ensure alignment.

Subsection 3.2: Regular Check-Ins and Adjustments

Check-ins foster unity. We explore the benefits of regular discussions about parenting challenges, triumphs, and areas for improvement.

Subsection 3.3: Maintaining Intimacy Amid Parenting Responsibilities

Maintaining intimacy is essential. We delve into strategies for prioritizing the couple's relationship amid the demands of parenting, ensuring emotional connection.

In this chapter, we've illuminated the intricacies of parenthood as a joint adventure and how it affects marital dynamics. By embracing co-parenting, sharing responsibilities, and nurturing open communication, couples can navigate the challenges of raising a family while maintaining their unity as a team. As we continue our journey, we'll uncover practical exercises and strategies that empower couples to thrive as parents, ensuring that their partnership remains strong and harmonious throughout the parenting journey.

11

Weathering Challenges and Celebrating Triumphs

Life is a blend of challenges and triumphs, and facing them as a united front strengthens the marital bond. In this chapter, we explore strategies for supporting each other through challenges and setbacks, as well as ways to celebrate achievements and milestones as a marital team.

Section 1: Supporting Each Other Through Challenges

Subsection 1.1: Recognizing Challenges as Opportunities for Growth
   Challenges are growth opportunities. We discuss how viewing setbacks as chances to learn and evolve shifts the perspective from defeat to resilience.

Subsection 1.2: Providing Emotional Support During Difficult Times
   Emotional support is essential. We explore ways to offer comfort, understanding, and empathy when one partner faces personal or external challenges.

Section 2: Strategies for Overcoming Challenges Together

Subsection 2.1: Open Communication About Difficulties

Communication eases burdens. We delve into the importance of discussing challenges openly, seeking solutions collaboratively, and avoiding blame.

Subsection 2.2: Leveraging Strengths to Overcome Obstacles

Strengths fortify the partnership. We discuss how identifying each partner's strengths and utilizing them to tackle challenges fosters a sense of unity.

Subsection 2.3: Seeking External Help When Needed

Seeking help is a sign of strength. We explore the value of seeking professional assistance or advice when facing challenges that require expertise.

Section 3: Celebrating Triumphs and Milestones

Subsection 3.1: Embracing a Culture of Celebration

Celebration nurtures positivity. We discuss how creating a culture of celebration in the relationship, both big and small, fosters joy and togetherness.

Subsection 3.2: Acknowledging Personal and Shared Achievements

Acknowledgment deepens connection. We explore how celebrating personal achievements and shared milestones reinforces the idea of being a supportive team.

Subsection 3.3: Rituals of Celebration and Gratitude

Rituals enhance connection. We delve into the significance of creating rituals to mark achievements, express gratitude, and reinforce the sense of unity.

In this chapter, we've illuminated the importance of weathering challenges and celebrating triumphs together. By providing emotional support, communicating openly, and leveraging each other's strengths, couples can navigate difficulties and emerge stronger. Additionally, celebrating achievements and embracing a culture of joy fosters a sense of unity and appreciation. As we move forward, we'll uncover practical exercises and strategies that empower couples to navigate challenges and celebrate their journey as a united and resilient team.

12

The Ongoing Journey of "We"

Marriage is an ever-evolving journey marked by growth, challenges, and continued commitment. In this final chapter, we reflect on the ongoing nature of this journey and explore strategies for nurturing and maintaining a strong partnership over the long term.

Section 1: Embracing the Fluid Nature of Marriage

Subsection 1.1: The Ever-Changing Landscape of Partnership
Marriage is dynamic, not static. We discuss how acknowledging the fluid nature of relationships encourages ongoing adaptation and growth.

Subsection 1.2: Embracing the Cycles of Connection
Relationships go through cycles. We explore the idea of cycles of closeness and distance, and how these natural shifts can be navigated with understanding and patience.

Section 2: Strategies for Nurturing Ongoing Connection

Subsection 2.1: Continuously Investing in Communication

Communication remains vital. We discuss the importance of continually honing communication skills and maintaining the practice of active listening and open dialogue.

Subsection 2.2: Making Time for Each Other Amid Busy Lives

Prioritizing time strengthens bonds. We delve into techniques for carving out quality time even when life gets busy, ensuring that the partnership remains central.

Subsection 2.3: Engaging in Lifelong Learning

Learning sustains growth. We explore the value of individually and collectively seeking personal development, which enriches the partnership over time.

Section 3: Sustaining Intimacy and Connection

Subsection 3.1: Keeping the Flame of Passion Alive

Passion requires nurturing. We discuss creative ways to maintain physical and emotional intimacy, ensuring that the romantic spark continues to burn.

Subsection 3.2: Celebrating Anniversaries and Milestones

Milestones are opportunities for reflection. We delve into the significance of celebrating anniversaries and reflecting on the journey together.

Subsection 3.3: The Power of Shared Dreams and Goals

Shared dreams inspire unity. We explore how continuously setting and pursuing shared goals keeps the partnership aligned and forward-looking.

In this final chapter, we've explored the ongoing journey of marriage and how to sustain a strong partnership over time. By embracing the ever-changing nature of relationships, nurturing ongoing connection, and maintaining intimacy and shared goals, couples can ensure that their journey from "Me" to "We" remains vibrant and fulfilling. As we conclude this book, we've laid the foundation for a lasting partnership built on communication, unity, and the journey of continuous growth.

Conclusion: From Me to We: A Guide to Marriage

The journey from "Me" to "We" is a transformative voyage that takes two individuals and weaves them into a harmonious partnership. Throughout the chapters of this guide, we've embarked on an exploration of the intricacies, joys, challenges, and triumphs that accompany this remarkable journey.

Marriage is a dynamic tapestry woven from the threads of communication, empathy, shared experiences, and mutual growth. It is a journey that requires continuous effort, adaptability, and a commitment to nurturing the bond that unites two souls.

As we reflect on the pages of this guide, we're reminded that the path to a strong and enduring partnership is marked by understanding, support, and the celebration of both individuality and togetherness. From laying the foundation of unity and shared goals to weathering challenges and celebrating triumphs, every step contributes to the masterpiece that is a successful marriage.

Remember that the journey doesn't end here. It's an ongoing adventure, a dance of connection that continues to evolve. Embrace change, communicate openly, and above all, nurture the love that brought you together.

From the initial spark of romance to the deep connection forged through life's changes, "From Me to We: A Guide to Marriage" serves as a roadmap, a companion, and a source of inspiration for the beautiful journey you've embarked upon. May your partnership continue to thrive, grow, and blossom, creating a tapestry of love, unity, and shared dreams that will stand the test of time.

With heartfelt wishes for a lifetime of joy, connection, and love,
[Your Name]

www.ingramcontent.com/pod-product-compliance
Lightning Source LLC
LaVergne TN
LVHW010440070526
838199LV00066B/6110